Our World of Information

Put It Together

Using Information

Claire Throp

Heinemann Library,
Chicago, IL

www.heinemannraintree.com
Visit our website to find out more information about Heinemann-Raintree books.

To order:
☎ Phone 888-454-2279
🖥 Visit www.heinemannraintree.com to browse our catalog and order online.

©2010 Heinemann Library
an imprint of Capstone Global Library, LLC
Chicago, Illinois

All rights reserved. No part of this publication may be reproduced or transmitted in any form or by any means, electronic or mechanical, including photocopying, recording, taping, or any information storage and retrieval system, without permission in writing from the publisher.

Edited by Rebecca Rissman and Catherine Veitch
Designed by Richard Parker
Original illustrations © Capstone Global Library
Illustrated by Darren Lingard
Picture research by Ruth Blair
Production by Duncan Gilbert
Originated by Heinemann Library
Printed in China by South China Printing Company Ltd.

14 13 12 11 10
10 9 8 7 6 5 4 3 2

Library of Congress Cataloging-in-Publication Data
Throp, Claire.
    Put it together : using information / Claire Throp.
        p. cm. -- (Our world of information)
    Includes bibliographical references and index.
    ISBN 978-1-4329-3373-9 -- ISBN 978-1-4329-3379-1 (pbk.)
1. Information resources--Juvenile literature. 2. Research--Methodology--Juvenile literature. 3. Report writing--Juvenile literature. I. Title.
    ZA3070.T483 2009
    020--dc22
                            2009004407

Acknowledgments

We would like to thank the following for permission to reproduce photographs: Alamy pp. **8** (© Tetra Images), **11** (© Ian Shaw), **17** (© Blackout Concepts), **21** (© Pablo Paul), **24** (© Vikki Martin); © Capstone Publishers pp. **10 & 14** (Karon Dubke); Corbis pp. **5** (Tom Stewart), **6** (LWA-JDC), **13**, **15** (LWA-Dann Tardif/Zefa), **28** (Jutta Klee); Getty Images pp. **18** (Tim Platt), **22** (Elyse Lewin), **25**; iStockphoto p. **26**; Photoshot p. **23** (Blend Images); Shutterstock p. **27** (© Dmitriy Shironosov).

Cover photograph of a child using a computer for schoolwork reproduced with permission of Corbis (Jose Luis Pelaez, Inc.).

Every effort has been made to contact copyright holders of any material reproduced in this book. Any omissions will be rectified in subsequent printings if notice is given to the publisher.

All the Internet addresses (URLs) given in this book were valid at the time of going to press. However, due to the dynamic nature of the Internet, some addresses may have changed, or sites may have changed or ceased to exist since publication. While the author and publisher regret any inconvenience this may cause readers, no responsibility for any such changes can be accepted by either the author or the publisher.

Contents

Any words appearing in the text in bold, **like this**, are explained in the glossary.

What Is Information?

 How many different **sources** of information can you see here?

You are surrounded by information. Information is what people know about things. It can be **sign language**, photographs, words, or many other things. Information can be used for talks and presentations, **projects**, and finding out about hobbies.

People use information in different ways. You might need to use information for a school assignment, for example. Or you might want to share information that you have found with friends, family, and your class.

 You can find a lot of information in books.

When Do You Need To Use Information?

There are many times that you will need to use information. You will need to use information for school assignments.

 School is a great place for finding and using information.

If you travel to a new place, you might look at **maps** before you go. When you are nearly there, you might ask someone for **directions**. The map and directions help you get where you want to go.

Listening

 Writing information down can help you remember it.

When you are being told information, good listening skills are important. If you do not **concentrate** when someone is telling you something, you may forget what they have said or not use the information correctly.

Sometimes you have to use information you are given right away. If you ask someone how to do something, you need to listen carefully. You may even need to write notes so you can use the information correctly.

 You may need to ask more questions after you get an answer.

Doing an Assignment

What was school like when your grandparents were young?

Always check that you have written down your assignment correctly.

For schoolwork, you need to make sure that you find the right information for whatever assignment or **project** you are doing. You can use a system to help you organize information. One idea is to break down the assignment or project into several parts.

 Breaking down an assignment helps you understand what it means.

Think about what you want to say or write for each part. Then look at the information you have. For example, your main assignment might be, "Find out what school was like 50 years ago." You could break this down into different parts, such as what the classroom was like, what schoolbooks were like, and what kinds of things children learned.

No Copying!

 Will you learn anything from copying someone else's work?

When something has been **published**, the information in it belongs to the writer or to the publisher. If someone else copies exactly the same words, it is the same as stealing a person's belongings.

You can use books, the Internet, and other **sources** of information to find general ideas and facts. If you need to use the exact words you find, make sure to say where those words came from and who wrote them.

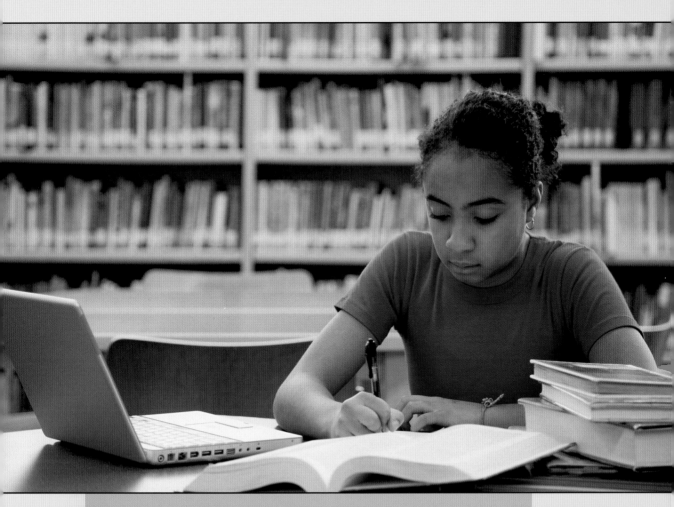

 When you use information, you must make sure that you do not steal other people's work.

Understanding Information

One of the best ways to avoid copying other people's work is to use a range of **sources**. You could find out about the same thing from a book, Website, television program, and a newspaper or magazine. Using a range of sources allows you **cross-check** facts and make sure they are correct.

 If you find it difficult to rewrite information in your own words, it may be that you do not fully understand it.

If you do not understand some information, ask an adult for help. Your teacher or a librarian will be able to talk things through with you, so you have a clear understanding of the information in your mind.

An adult can help you find a source of information that makes sense to you.

Using Pictures

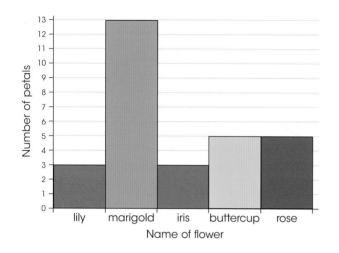

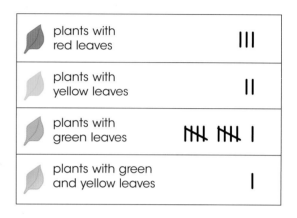

	plants with red leaves	III
	plants with yellow leaves	II
	plants with green leaves	ᴴᴴ ᴴᴴ I
	plants with green and yellow leaves	I

Tables and bar charts can help organize information.

Using pictures can make your work more useful and interesting. You can include charts, tables, and other **graphic organizers**. Photos and drawings can also be full of information. Try taking photos by yourself, or ask an adult to help you.

For example, you might have been given a school **project** on the life cycle of sunflowers. You could take photos of a seed, a small plant beginning to grow, a sunflower fully grown, and finally a sunflower dying.

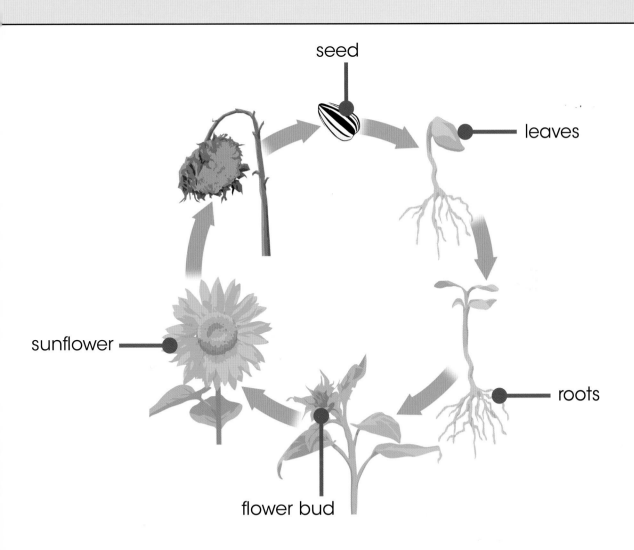

seed

leaves

sunflower

roots

flower bud

Spoken Information

Sometimes you might want to use an object to present information to your class. For example, an old photo of a classroom would help you explain to your friends what school was like in the past.

You can share information in a group discussion.

Your teacher shares information with you and the rest of your class every day. The main way that your teacher does this is by talking to you and telling you what he or she knows.

 You, too, can share information by talking to your class.

Online Information

If you are working with several people on a **project**, you can use the Internet to share information. You could do this by using **instant messaging**. You could also use a **wiki**. This is a Website that allows several people to add or change information.

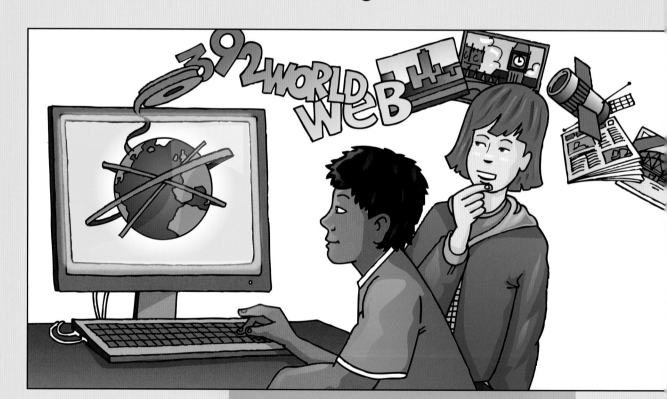

 You can send your part of a project to friends as an **Email** attachment.

You should only open Email attachments or share information online if you know who or where it is from. Attachments from friends and family are usually safe.

Be careful when opening Email attachments.

Making Choices

You can use information to help you make choices. If you are trying to decide whether to start a new hobby, you could find out about it online. You could also ask friends who have the same hobby what they think about it.

Friends can be a good source of information.

Decisions such as where to go on vacation can be difficult. Your family may read about places to go on vacation in a magazine. You could also pay a visit to the library and use their **online catalog** to find information **sources**, such as books about different places.

 After reading all the information, you and your family can decide where you would like to visit.

Other Ways to Use Information

Information can be put together in special ways. People who are visually impaired use a system of writing called Braille. It uses raised dots that stand for letters and numbers.

 People who are deaf may use **sign language**, a system of hand movements that stand for spoken words.

Sometimes meetings take place where people speak different **languages**. Someone who can speak several languages is called an **interpreter**. He or she **translates** what is being said, so that everyone can understand what is going on.

 People wear earpieces that allow them to them to hear an interpreter.

Sharing Information

 You can find information quickly if you work with others.

Information can be used in many ways. You might need to use it for group **projects** at school. You might use information to help you make decisions.

Communicating with other people is an important way to use information. Sharing information that you have found helps everybody learn new things.

 Information can be used to tell others how you feel about something.

27

Activities

Best Friend Poster

Make a poster about your best friend. You could put their name at the top and then include some photos of them. Write captions for each photo to explain what is happening in the picture or how old your friend was at the time. You could even put the pictures in time order. This is called a **timeline**.

Rewriting Practice

Copying other people's work is wrong. It is a good idea to practice putting information into your own words. Read the following two pieces of text about recycling. Then try to rewrite the information using your own words.

People use different materials, such as paper, glass, metal, and plastic, every day. These materials are very useful, but sometimes they are wasted. When you throw materials away you make waste. Recycling is when people change waste items into things that can be used again. You should recycle as much as possible to help care for the planet. Separate your glass bottles from newspaper and cans. Many cities and towns have recycling trucks that pick up your recycling every week.

Things that can be recycled:

- paper
- cards
- aluminum foil
- cans
- glass bottles
- plastic bottles
- newspapers and magazines

Glossary

communicate share information or ideas

concentrate think about one particular thing at a time

cross-check checking a particular piece of information in a number of sources

directions explanation for how to get to a certain place or how to do something

Email electronic mail. Email messages are sent from one computer to another.

graphic organizer way of showing information in a chart, table, or graph

instant messaging way of talking to other people through connected computers. It is different from Email because it happens as though you were talking face-to-face.

interpreter person who can speak different languages and tells other people what is being said so that they can understand

language set of words that people use to share information. People in different countries use different words, but they mean the same thing.

map picture of a particular area, such as a town, that shows where things are. A map often includes roads, streets, parks, and important buildings.

online catalog electronic list of all the information sources, such as books, movies, and magazines, that can be found in a particular library. The list can be accessed by computer.

project task set by a teacher that can be done on your own or with other people

published printed materials, such as books and magazines, produced for sale

sign language system of hand movements that stand for spoken words

source place in which we can find things such as information. Books, television, and Websites on the Internet are sources of information.

timeline arrangement of pictures or text in the order they happened in time

translate to change from one language to another

wiki Website that allows many people to add or change information

Find Out More

Books

Hoena, B.A. *The Library*. Mankato, Minn.: Capstone Press, 2004.

Oxlade, Chris. *My First Internet Guide*. Chicago, Ill.: Heinemann Library, 2007.

Websites

Homework Help – Yahoo! Kids
http://kids.yahoo.com/learn
This web page includes links to an encyclopedia, dictionary, maps, and a lot of other useful Websites.

Ask Kids – Schoolhouse
www.askkids.com/schoolhouse?pch=sch
Ask Kids is a great search engine specially created for use by children.

BBC – Students
www.bbc.co.uk/schools/students/
This Website includes many different activities and games to help you learn.

Index